P9-ECV-063

Mainfränkisches Museum Würzburg

Riemenschneider Collection

Text by Claudia Lichte
Introduction by Hans-Peter Trenschel
Photos by Rolf Nachbar

Prestel

Munich · London · New York

Contents

Above: Woman on a chandelier, Tilman Riemenschneider, c. 1515

Right: Figures made for the Würzburg Lady Chapel, in the Riemenschneider Room of the Mainfränkisches Museum

The nucleus and main attraction of the Mainfränkisches Museum in Würzburg is its unique collection of works by Tilman Riemenschneider. Comprising eighty-one sculptures and carvings by the master himself, by his workshop, his school and his circle, it is the largest collection of its kind in the world. The depth and diversity of this body of work distinguish it from collections in other museums, some of which possess outstanding figures by Riemenschneider, none of which, however, can fully illustrate the far-reaching influence exerted by the work of this Würzburg sculptor in Franconia.

The origins of this collection go back to the 19th century, and it has continued to grow in the course of time. Like the Mainfränkisches Museum itself, the collection of works by Riemenschneider and his circle was the outcome of a union of three other collections: from the Historischer Verein (Historical Society) of Lower Franconia and Aschaffenburg, founded in 1831; from the City of Würzburg; and from the Fränkischer Kunst- und Altertumsverein (Franconian Society for Art and Early History), founded in 1893.

The rediscovery of Riemenschneider can be attributed to Karl Gottfried Scharold, a legation counsellor and the first and long-time director of the Historischer Verein. It is understandable, therefore, that from the very beginning this society was interested in acquiring works by the Würzburg master for its collections. In addition, over a period of many decades, it was entrusted with works that could not be left safely in their original locations. This applies especially to Riemenschneider's figures from the Lady Chapel in Würzburg, and to the famous statues of Adam and Eve.

Encouraged by the example of the Historischer Verein, the City of Würzburg began to enlarge its own art collections. Works by Riemenschneider already in its possession and from associated institutions were brought together by the city in a single location. Further purchases were also made as funds allowed.

The Fränkischer Kunst- und Altertumsverein had two main objectives: to collect Franconian art and cultural artefacts and to found a museum in which the various art collections in Würzburg could be united. The Franconian Luitpold Museum was opened in 1913. In 1939 its name was changed to 'Mainfränkisches Museum Würzburg'. The Historischer Verein contributed thirty works by Riemenschneider, his workshop and his circle to the collections in the new museum, the City of Würzburg twenty pieces and the Fränkischer Kunst- und Altertumsverein eleven sculptures.

It was possible to assemble the most important Riemenschneider works from these collections in a single room. Other works, attributed to his workshop and school, were exhibited in two additional rooms. This arrangement soon proved unsatisfactory, however. The situation was redressed by the erection of the Riemenschneider Room, which was designed by Clemens Schenk and opened in 1931. With the figures of Adam and Eve occupying a central position, the most valuable exhibits of the museum found a fitting home.

The air raid on Würzburg on 16 March 1945 completely destroyed the museum building in Maxstrasse. Most of the Riemenschneider collection had been removed elsewhere for safe keeping and was thereby safe from destruction; but the figures of the Apostles from the Lady Chapel, which were attached to the walls of the museum and therefore had not been removed, were broken into many pieces. It proved possible, however, to salvage the fragments and subsequently restore these works. Eleven wood carvings by the Riemenschneider workshop, his school and his circle were irretrievably lost.

The catastrophe of 1945 led to the idea of re-establishing the museum on the fortified Marienberg. This was achieved by Max H. von Freeden under extremely difficult conditions. One of the first rooms to be completed, in 1947, was the Riemenschneider Room, and the figures of Adam and Eve – surrounded by the other works of the Riemenschneider Collection – again formed the main visual attraction of this large, pillared space.

The existing collection was subsequently enlarged by the addition of twenty-one sculptures and carvings, including a work of such outstanding importance as the great stone Madonna from Riemenschneider's late period. As a result, the collection became too large for the space, and it was no longer possible to present the exhibits in a fitting manner. New developments in security, climate-control and lighting technology also demonstrated the need for a modernization of the museum.

After exhaustive planning and a nine-month transitional period, the newly designed Riemenschneider Room was reopened to the public on 21 July 1998. The grouping of the small sculptures in four large all-glass, air-conditioned showcases left adequate space along the walls to display the larger wood and stone sculptures. The rear part of the room broadens for the presentation of the finest objects in the collection: the figures of Adam and Eve flanked by the Apostles from the buttresses of the Lady Chapel, as well as the Virgin Mourning from Acholshausen and the large stone figure of the Virgin Mary. An appropriate lighting design coupled with new lighting techniques enable these masterpieces to be seen in all their glory.

c. 1460	Born in Eichsfeld, Heiligen-stadt
1478–79	First stay in Würzburg
1483	Apprentice in Würzburg. Becomes member of the painters' Guild of St Luke
1485	First marriage, to Anna Schmidt. Becomes freeman of the city and master in Würzburg. Workshop in the courtyard of 'zum Wolfmanns-ziechlein' in Franziskanergasse

1490	Commissioned to execute St Mary Magdalene altarpiece in Münnerstadt, erected in 1493
1491	Commissioned to execute Adam and Eve on market portal of Würzburg Lady Chapel, completed in 1493
1496	Commissioned to execute funerary monument for Prince-Bishop Rudolf von Scherenberg in Würzburg Cathedral, erected in 1513

1497	Second marriage, to Anna Rappolt
1499	Commissioned to execute Emperor's tomb in Bamberg Cathedral, erected in 1513
c. 1500–5	Passion Cycle altarpiece for Dominican Church in Rothen-burg, now in Detwang

1501	Commissioned to execute the Holy Blood altarpiece in the city parish church of St James in Rothenburg ob der Tauber, delivered in 1502 and 1504/5
1504	Appointed to Würzburg Lower Town Council, member until 1525

Anno dm̄ · M · cccc · xxxi · am

abent Kiliani starb der Erſam vnd Kunſtreich Tilman

Anno · Dm̄ · M · D · xli · den · xxiii
tag · des · brachmons · iſt · verſchi
den · der · Erſam · Bernhard · hap
koffſchuldes · hie · zu · wirczburg
leidt · bey · ſeinem · ſchwaier · vnder
dem · ſtein · denn · got
gnat · amen ·

rieger · zu · wirczburg · dem · got · gnedig · ſey · Amen

1 | ## Tombstone of Tilman Riemenschneider
Jörg Riemenschneider, 1531
From Würzburg Cathedral graveyard
Red sandstone; height: 204 cm; width: 96 cm
Friends of Mainfrankish Art and History,
Inv. No. H. 42 566

Renowned far beyond the confines of Würzburg during his lifetime, Tilman Riemenschneider passed into oblivion after his death on 7 July 1531. His rediscovery began when his gravestone came to light during construction work carried out between the Cathedral and the New Minster in 1822. On the slab Riemenschneider is depicted wearing the costume of a 16th-century freeman of the city. Between his feet is a speaking coat of arms with carved straps. The surrounding inscription reads: 'Anno dm [domini] 1531 on St Kilian's Eve died Tilman Riemenschneider of great repute and talent, sculptor, freeman of Würzburg, to whom God be merciful, Amen.' On examining contemporaneous archive material, Karl Gottfried Scharold found frequent mention of the artist. In 1841 the first life of the Würzburg master was published, a biography still regarded as accurate in most details.

Tilman Riemenschneider's tombstone was probably made by his son Jörg, who took over his father's workshop. Tilman's son-in-law, Bernhard Hop, was commemorated ten years later on the same gravestone. The field containing the inscription to him was chiselled into the full-length representation of Riemenschneider. 'Recycling' the slab in this cavalier manner demonstrates all too clearly that Riemenschneider was not honoured with a burial commensurate with his status as an artist.

FIGURES FOR THE WÜRZBURG LADY CHAPEL

2 – 3

Adam and Eve

Tilman Riemenschneider, 1492–93

From the south portal of the Würzburg Lady Chapel

Grey sandstone from Königsberg (Hassberge Dist.);
height: 189 and 186 cm

Surface partly worked over, additions to Adam's right arm and
feet and to Eve's right foot with serpent

Marienkapellenstiftung Würzburg, Inv. No. Lg. 32 060, 32 061

In November 1490 the Würzburg Town Council decided to replace the old figures of Adam and Eve flanking the market portal of the Lady Chapel and to fill the still empty niches high above on the buttresses with sculpture. In May 1491 Tilman Riemenschneider was commissioned to start on the portal sculpture with its associated consoles and baldachins. This was his first public commission in Würzburg. Well into September 1493 he was still working on the figures of Adam and Eve, which number among his early masterpieces. Despite serious damage and numerous later additions, they are still impressive as consumate manifestations of an idealized yet naturalistic conception of the human body. Depicting Adam in this unusual

manner as a beardless youth required the express permission of the Town Council, which resolved *in camera* on 21 December 1492 'that the man Adam hewn by Master Tyll in stone may have no beard'. The fine grain of the grey sandstone made it possible to carve subtly modulated forms. The arch of Adam's ribcage, for example, is clearly delineated. Eve appears as a young woman with broad hips and a slender torso. In her right hand she holds the apple from the Tree of Knowledge; the serpent writhes round her right foot. Facial features, such as almond-shaped, slightly slanted eyes with narrow upper and lower lids contained in the curve of the brows, evoke a sweet and gentle sentiment, which is a salient characteristic of all work by Riemenschneider's own

hand. The full lips, the soft curves of the cheeks, the very slight dimples on the figures' chins and the delicately carved strands of curly or wavy hair attest to the sculptor's meticulous handling of his medium in all details.

The Würzburg Town Council acknowledged the artist's superb work by remunerating him well for it. On granting the commission, the Council had settled on a fee of 100 guilders for Riemenschneider. 'Should he, however, execute the above with such masterly and consummate artistry that a Town Council can recognize that he has well earned it, he may be given 120 guilders.' Even though the fee included the execution of consoles and balda-chins for the figures, it nevertheless indicates how highly regarded the work was. By contrast, only 10 guilders were paid for each of the Apostle figures along the Lady Chapel, which were executed between 1500 and 1506 in Riemenschneider's workshop.

In 1894 Adam and Eve were removed from the south portal of the Lady Chapel 'because of their nudity'. Today copies stand in their place.

4 St Jude (Thaddaeus)

Workshop of Tilman Riemenschneider, 1500–6

From a buttress of the Würzburg Lady Chapel

Grey sandstone from Königsberg (Hassberge Dist.), addition to nose; height: 187 cm

Marienkapellenstiftung Würzburg, Inv. No. Lg. 32 076

On granting their first commission in 1490 to Riemenschneider, the Würzburg Councilmen had hinted at another to execute 'other figures' on the Lady Chapel. In 1492 the commission was couched in more explicit terms: the still empty niches for figures on the buttresses well above eye-level were to be filled with an Apostle cycle (No. 5). The first blocks of stone for the figure cycle had been quarried by 1492. In 1497 and 1499 the stone was transported to Würzburg. A year later Riemenschneider's workshop began work on what was to be fourteen figures: the twelve Apostles, John the Baptist and Christ were complete by 1506.

Because the buttress figures were originally placed so high up, their lower torsos were substantially foreshortened and the heads and hands were made to be seen from the worm's-eye view. These figures are less subtly carved than the statues of Adam and Eve, which were once placed so much lower. Riemenschneider himself executed the designs for the figures and certainly for the heads, which were highly expressive of individual character, but presumably left the execution for the most part to his workshop. An apprentice seems to have been at work on the statue of St Jude the Apostle, distinctive for its ruggedly angular features and the coarsely articulated, uniform sweep of its robe. Tilman Riemenschneider received a fee of only 10 guilders for each of these figures.

5 ### The Würzburg Lady Chapel
Peter Geist, *c.* 1845
Oil on canvas; 63 x 52 cm
City of Würzburg, Inv. No. S. 47 141

The painting shows the figures of Adam and Eve on the market portal and above them the Apostle cycle figures round the chapel in the buttress niches.

6 ### Head of St Bartholomew (detail)
Workshop of Tilman Riemenschneider, 1500–6
From a buttress of the Würzburg Lady Chapel
Grey sandstone from Königsberg (Hassberge Dist.);
overall height: 183 cm
Additions to nose and curls
Marienkapellenstiftung Würzburg, Inv. No. Lg. 32 077

The Apostle figures executed for the Würzburg Lady Chapel were originally placed high up in the buttress niches so that they could be viewed only from a distance. Consequently, St Bartholomew's head is framed with coarse hair in heavy strands. The cheekbones are prominent and the eyes are surrounded by deeply gouged wrinkles. Arched brows and a protruding lower lip lend the face a mantic expression. By reducing faces to salient features that seem exaggeratedly accentuated when viewed from close up, Riemenschneider and his workshop succeeded in individualizing figures so that each was distinctive and easily recognizable from far away.

7 | St Philip

Workshop of Tilman Riemenschneider, 1500–6

From a buttress of the Würzburg Lady Chapel

Grey sandstone from Königsberg (Hassberge Dist.);
height: 195 cm

Marienkapellenstiftung Würzburg, Inv. No. Lg. 32 079

In 1900 Eduard Tönnies described the Apostle figures executed by Tilman Riemenschneider and his workshop for the Würzburg Lady Chapel as 'simple burghers, whose occupations are not intellectual in nature, men who do not find thinking easy'. Indeed the stone figures do seem rather mundane. That St Philip is somewhat corpulent is emphasized by his belt having slipped a little below his bulging belly. The features of his broad, slightly bloated face with its heavy double chin are distinctly individual. Despite the frequent claims to the contrary, this is probably not a portrait of Martin Luther. What is represented is a well-fed, elderly man of the type depicted as a king wearing a turban in the Adoration of the Magi relief (No. 21). Moreover, the head of the middle king in the Adoration relief is not unlike that of St Bartholomew in the Würzburg Lady Chapel (No. 6). Apparently Riemenschneider developed specific types while working on early major commissions, such as the Apostle cycle. From then on, his workshop could replicate individualized character heads and schematic textile folds in varying contexts. Apprentices are likely to have worked after the master's models.

8 | St John Mourning
Tilman Riemenschneider, *c.* 1490
Limewood, retaining most of the original gesso, originally
worked in the round; height: 116 cm
Friends of Mainfrankish Art and History,
Inv. No. H. 14 166

By the time Tilman Riemenschneider arrived in
Würzburg in 1483, he had completed his training
as a sculptor. Here he worked in both wood and stone.
Although there is no record of where Riemenschneider
served his apprenticeship, it has been variously sug
gested on the basis of his early work that he trained in
Thuringia, in the Netherlands, in Ulm or on the upper
reaches of the Rhine.

St John Mourning is an early Riemenschneider from
an otherwise unknown Crucifixion group that has retained most of the original paint. The figure's plasticity
is impressive. The weight-bearing leg is counterbal-
anced by a flexed left leg in a forward step, which is
clearly delineated beneath the figure's heavy cloak.
Shell-like, John's cloak, bunched under his forearm,
surrounds his body to fall in radiating folds, exposing
the garment beneath it in a deep cleft. In the last third
of the 15th century clothing draped in this sophisticated manner was as typical of sculpture from the upper
reaches of the Rhine as were softly modulated facial
features and delicately chiselled locks of hair. Upper
Rhenish sculpture was strongly influenced by the
Netherlandish sculptor Nicolaus Gerhaert van Leyden,
who spent quite some time between 1463 and 1467 in
Strasbourg. Netherlandish influence is also conspicu-
ous in sculpture of this period from Ulm. The complex
inter-relationship between the Upper Rhenish workshops and those in Ulm and in the Netherlands has
yet to be disentangled. However, the high degree of
plasticity, which is such a distinctive feature of early
Riemenschneider's, such as St John, would suggest that
the Würzburg master trained on the upper reaches of
the Rhine and/or in Ulm.

9   Virgin and Child

Tilman Riemenschneider, c. 1490

From a house in Merkershausen (Rhön-Grabfeld Dist.)
Limewood (?), originally worked in the round, surface
severely damaged; height: 91 cm
On loan from private collection, Inv. No. Lg. 62 171

The severe damage the Madonna has sustained allows only a hint of the quality that originally distinguished the figure to shine through. A continuous S-curve runs through the work, structuring the composition. The Virgin is holding the infant Christ on her left arm. Her left hand draws up her cloak, which falls from there in a round sweep across her body. The Virgin's right arm originally crossed her torso to support the Christ Child. The softly modulated faces of the Virgin and Child gaze into an indeterminate distance. Comparable compositions are known from Upper Rhenish figures dating from the last third of the 15th century. Riemenschneider's early work in particular reveals definitive similarities with them.

The fragmentary condition of the work vividly attests to a turbulent history. The Madonna was originally a free-standing figure, mounted on a round tenon so that she could be viewed from all sides. The tip of her cloak swung out crisply to define the outer limits of her clothing. The tip was later sawed off to give the figure a stable base. Probably during the Baroque period the Virgin's hair and ears as well as those of the Child were smoothed over, presumably so that the heads might be decorated with wigs and crowns to suit the prevailing taste. In addition, the figure must have been exposed to wind and weather for quite some time, as its brittle surface and the crack in the Virgin's head would seem to indicate. The Madonna seems to have been long forgotten before being rediscovered in the attic of a private house in Merkershausen and loaned to the Mainfränkisches Museum in 1976.

10 The Virgin and Child with St Anne
Tilman Riemenschneider, *c.* 1495

From Kitzingen

Grey sandstone; height: 79 cm

Friends of Mainfrankish Art and History,
Inv. No. A. 32 640

St Anne is seated, holding her daughter, the Virgin, and the infant Christ on her lap. Lost in thought, the Virgin is reading a book, presumably the Old Testament, which reveals to her the birth of the Redeemer. The infant Christ is standing, supporting himself with one hand on Anne's breast. In the other he holds a pear.

That the stone sculpture was originally intended to grace an octagonal pier is attested to by an approx. 120-degree-angle obtuse recess on the back. This means that the group is in three-quarters relief rather than in the round. The Christ Child is free-standing, a device which opens up new views into and perspectives on the composition. Dating this superb work, which has always been attributed to Riemenschneider himself, has been the subject of vehement controversy. Some art historians view it as a late work, dating from about 1520, because of its harmonious composition and the elegaic serenity it radiates. Others, however, classify it as an early work of the master on the grounds of its high degree of plasticity and the broad surfaces of the garment folds. Indeed, the staggered layering of planes suggesting depth, the generous folds of St Anne's robe and above all the soft yet subtle handling of the bodies and faces, recalling the sophisticated modulation of Adam and Eve on the Würzburg Cathedral market portal (Nos. 2 and 3), would suggest a date of about 1495. The existence of numerous replicas in wood from Riemenschneider's workshop and circle drawing on this composition make it all the more likely that this is an early work.

11 Virgin and Child

Tilman Riemenschneider, *c.* 1500

Limewood (?), back finished in the round; height: 29.9 cm

City of Würzburg, Inv. No. S. 49 792

Because such meticulous attention has been paid to detail even on the back, this little figure of the Virgin invites close scrutiny. The unusual plasticity of both body and garment continually reveals entirely new perspectives when the statuette is turned. Consequently, this little Madonna seems almost like a collector's item that once graced a Kunstkammer, so entirely does it lend itself to direct communion with the spectator. This statuette of the Virgin may have

served as a model in Riemenschneider's workshop, for some extant figures take up and repeat the composition on a larger scale. Use as a model would not, however, preclude final deployment to a different context altogether. It was probably destined for domestic use, where it would have been the subject of contemplative private devotions.

Crucifix (detail)

Tilman Riemenschneider, *c.* 1500

Limewood (?), worked fully in the round, arms attached with
dowels, gesso leached off; overall height: 43 cm

City of Würzburg, Inv. No. S. 43 504

Riemenschneider and his workshop made a number
of crucifixes of varying sizes that were intended to
be positioned in a variety of places. Oval faces express
the sufferings of Christ in knit brows, deep-set eyes
with drooping upper lids, emphatic cheekbones and
slightly open mouths with relaxed lower jaws.

Two little crucifixes (43 and 29 cm) in the Würzburg
Mainfränkisches Museum are thought to have been
workshop models. Indeed, the larger of the two crucifixes, shown here, reveals varying degrees of finish,
ranging from the carefully smoothed ribcage with inlaid nipples, the ruggedly angular and expressively
carved face to locks of hair, which are in places only
coarsely defined. The lack of uniformity in finish and
the similarity in composition with crucifixes on a
larger scale, such as the crucifix in Eising parish
church, would suggest that this was used as a model.
However, the original surface finish has been subjected
repeatedly to drastic interventions so that it is no
longer possible even to determine whether this crucifix
was originally painted. The gesso and the manner in
which the crucifix was to be positioned may have been
part of the original conception. Like the statuette of
the Virgin (No. 11), this crucifix may have been part of
a free-standing Crucifixion group or a Crucifixion in
an altar shrine for use in personal devotions. Neither
use would preclude its having served as a model.

13

Crucifix
Workshop of Tilman Riemenschneider, *c.* 1515–20

From the Chapel of the Holy Spirit in the Bürgerspital,
Würzburg
Limewood (?), probably originally polychromed, worked fully in
the round, additions to the cross; height: 100 cm
Loaned by the Würzburg Bürgerspital, Inv. No. Lg. 40 110

This crucifix, which is one metre high, was made to be placed high above eye-level. The drooping head, the solid foreshortened body and the simplicity in the rendering of detail indicate that it was to be viewed from quite a distance.

The crucifix clearly reveals the rationalized handling characteristic of the Riemenschneider workshop: Christ's body, head and legs were made from one tree trunk. The arms were added, as were the dangling ends of the loincloth and the front of the right foot – all parts that exceeded the dimensions of the block of wood used. The arms of the Christ figure were applied with dowels – a readily discernible method in the small crucifix (No. 12) whose joints were later broken out along the edges.

It is difficult to ascertain the dates of the crucifixes made by Riemenschneider and his workshop because the type of representation and handling hardly changed over the decades. The dates of only two extant crucifixes are irrefutable: the crucifix made in 1497 for the Würzburg Cathedral chancel arch, of which a plaster cast of the face is extant (No. 14), and the crucifix in Steinach an der Saale dating from 1516. If one postulates a development from what was probably a slender, elongated representation of the body to a sturdier one, the Crucified from the Chapel of the Holy Spirit in the Würzburg Bürgerspital would be assigned to Riemenschneider's later work. The bodily proportions and the angle from which the work was to be viewed tally with the place for which it would originally have been designed.

14

Plaster cast taken from the face of Christ on the crucifix once on the chancel arch of Würzburg Cathedral

Original: Tilman Riemenschneider, 1497,
destroyed in 1945

Plaster cast: Andreas Halbig, c. 1850–60

Friends of Mainfrankish Art and History,
Inv. No. H. 7 410

The wooden crucifix on the chancel arch of Würzburg Cathedral was 3.5 m tall. Destroyed by fire in 1945 when Würzburg went up in flames, it is only known to us from old photographs and from a plaster cast of the face.

A letter of Indulgence, first made public in 1899 and found in the head of the Christ figure, was dated 1478 and an additional note bore the name Riemenschneider. The ensuing confusion was finally cleared up when a later generation of scholars discovered that the name was that of the Cathedral vicar, Nicolaus Riemenschneider, the sculptor's uncle, who signed for the Cathedral chapter. The letter of Indulgence referred to an earlier Crucifixion group. The chancel arch crucifix was not put in place until 1497, when the Prince-Bishop, Lorenz von Bibra, renewed the dispensation. On this occasion the old letter was placed in the head of the new crucifix.

The sculptor Andreas Halbig (1800–69) of Donnersdorf near Hassfurt probably made the plaster cast. He helped to remove the documents and relics from the head. The Nuremberg Germanisches Nationalmuseum presented the cast to the Historischer Verein in 1860.

Found in 1979 in the Mainfränkisches Museum magazine, the cast is notable as a monumental rendering of the formulaic Riemenschneider face with half-closed almond eyes, knit brows, a slightly open mouth and a protruding lower lip.

15

The Virgin Mourning

Tilman Riemenschneider, *c.* 1505

From a house in Acholshausen (Würzburg Dist.)

Limewood, polychromed, worked fully in the round;
height: 179 cm

City of Würzburg, Inv. No. S. 32 639

The Acholshausen Virgin Mourning is a special case
in the Riemenschneider Collection of wooden
sculpture. It is life-sized and its closed contours make it
seem monumental. The usual hollowing of the back
(see No. 16), which was to prevent the wooden block
from cracking, has been closed with a fitted panel. This
means that the figure was meant to be viewed from
the back as well as the front. The Virgin Mourning was
originally part of what is known as a Cross Triumph-
ant group, consisting of Christ on the Cross, the Virgin
and St John. The figures were placed high up in the
church vaulting on a beam, where the Virgin Mourning was below the right bar of the Cross. The Acholshausen Virgin has been subtly adapted to such an
angle of vision. The spectator is attracted to the large
face and hands as well as the sinuously dangling head
garment which plays about the figure's head and hands.

Side view of the Virgin
Mourning (detail). The loop,
by means of which the
figure was originally fastend
to the vaulting, and the
panel set into the back are
both visible

Her cloak disguises the elongation of the torso in flowing pleats that fall into uniform channels from her hips. The parts of the headscarf that have been carved fully in the round enliven the side views. Although the proportions of the figure indicate that it is to be viewed from a distance, details are sensitively and delicately worked out. The features of the gently rounded face are marked by quiet lamentation, the lifelessly dangling hands play unconsciously with the cloak. The figure's ankles, limbs, nails and facial wrinkles are all clearly discernible.The high quality of the workmanship is underscored by painting, which has remained largely intact. Restored in 1998, it glows in all its original brilliance. This is a second application of paint, laid over the original colour, without a fresh layer of ground. The grey and white of the scarf and the outside of the cloak, representing mourning in the Middle Ages, contrast sharply with the red lining. The blue dress, lined with green, is only visible on the breast and round the feet, and was originally decorated with appliqués. The cloak is trimmed with a gold border.

It is not known where this Virgin was originally placed. Her previous owner, Johann Valentin Markert, master beltmaker of Würzburg, wrote when she was discovered in 1895: 'One day Isaak Strauss of Gaukönigshofen came to me and said he had a large figure with particularly lovely hands. ... So I went to Gaukönigshofen. ... There I saw the Madonna tied to a door handle by a rope about her neck. Strauss said he would be willing to sell me the Madonna for 50 Marks. He had also had the St John which went with her. However, the latter figure was so wormeaten that he had chopped it up and thrown it on the fire. He had bought both figures in Acholshausen from Franz Pfeuffer, a peasant. There they had stood in the attic behind the chimney. The peasant had said to Strauss: "Just see you get those old chimney riders out of the house. My people are afraid of them." 'Known as 'The Witch', the figure is now regarded as an outstanding work from Riemenschneider's own hand.

Hands of the Virgin Mourning (detail)

16

St John Mourning

Tilman Riemenschneider, *c.* 1505

Limewood (?), originally polychromed, hollowed back;
height: 82 cm

City of Würzburg, Inv. No. S. 32 906

St John stands with his left foot slightly in front of his right and is holding a book with both hands. Over his ankle-length undergarment he wears a cloak, which falls across his body in broad, sweeping folds. This youthful St John, who wears a sorrowful expression, was probably once part of a Crucifixion group.

It probably stood in the central body of the altarpiece since the hollow in the back has not been closed as is the case with the Acholshausen Virgin Mourning (No. 15).

Most wooden sculpture in the Mainfränkisches Museum's Riemenschneider Collection originally stood in the shrines of winged altarpieces. This type of retable consisted of a frame with panels hinged at the sides, a 'predella' or plinth and a crowning finial. On weekdays the wings of the altarpiece were closed so that only the painted outer panels were displayed. On holy days the altarpiece was 'transformed', that is the shutters were opened out to reveal the magnificently worked interior with statues and reliefs (see illus. on p. 44). Three trades participated traditionally in making a winged altarpiece. A carpenter made the framework. The figures or reliefs for the shrine, predella,

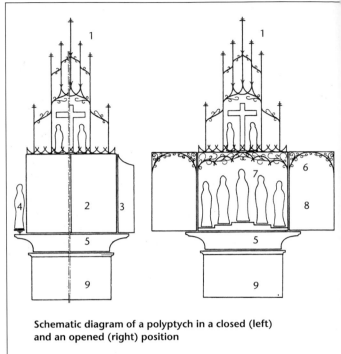

Schematic diagram of a polyptych in a closed (left) and an opened (right) position

1 Finial

2 Shrine, closed, outside wing panels visible

3 Fixed wing
   or
4 Guardian of the shrine

5 Predella (altar pedestal)

6 Baldachin / blind tracery

7 Shrine, opened, interior visible, frequently with statues

8 Inside of panels often with relief decoration

9 Altar table

finial and inside panels were carved by sculptors. Paintings on the panels and predella were executed by artists, who were often charged with painting the shrine and the works displayed there.

To prevent the wood splitting, sculptors hollowed out the backs of their figures. If the figures were placed before a closed back wall as in the main section of an altarpiece, the hollowed backs were invisible so that it was not necessary to close them with fitted panels.

The hollowed backs of the figures now in museums indicate that they were once placed in or on an altarpiece.

The sculpture of St John vividly documents how such figures were made. Apparently quite green, even damp, wood was used. This is shown in the numerous cracks that appeared while the wood was drying and in the black traces of soot in the hollows of the backs, which are probably the result of the sculpture being dried over the fire. The backs of the heads were not hollowed out so that this solid part tended to split while drying. The crack running through St John's left eye and on into the cheek was later planed smooth yet is still visible. Such repairs were originally covered over by size and paint (see No. 23). Tilman Riemenschneider was the first wood-carver of his time to make figures and reliefs that were not intended to be covered with several layers of paint. However, most of the pieces in the Mainfränkisches Museum's Riemenschneider Collection were, as recent tests have shown, originally coloured. Evidently, the Riemenschneider workshop executed wooden sculpture that was to be painted, even in the later period, and contemporaneously works in wood that were to be left upainted. If several layers of gesso were intended, the surface did not have to be finished as carefully by the sculptor. The last touches were left to the painter and sizer.

17

Angel holding a Candlestick
Workshop of Tilman Riemenschneider, *c*. 1505
Additions to the candlestick; height: 57 cm
City of Würzburg, Inv. No. S. 32 688

Kneeling and turning to the right, the angel is clothed in bishops' vestments and holds a candlestick with both hands. A mirror-image companion piece is also to be found in the Mainfränkisches Museum. Both figures have been worked in the round; nevertheless, the backs reveal only sketchy workmanship. These are works which were meant to be viewed from the side against a solid background.

The scultpure echoes the composition of the Angel with the column of the Flagellation from the predella of the Rothenburg Altarpiece of the Holy Blood, which Tilman Riemenschneider was commissioned to execut in 1501. The Angel holding a Candlestick is not so subtly modulated as the work it is modelled on, as its sharper facial features show. The Würzburg angels wer probably, therefore, made by a member of Riemenschneider's workshop. Like the Rothenburg angels the were modelled on, they were probably in the main body of an altarpiece, free-standing against a rear wall, or perhaps in a predella, flanking a reliquary.

The two angels with candlesticks were purchased in 1901 by the city of Würzburg for its collections. At that time they showed traces of paint, albeit probably not the original coat, which was soon afterwards removed. The unpainted Riemenschneider works in the Münnerstädt, Rothenburg and Creglingen altarpieces have been instrumental in shaping the modern idea of how the master's sculpture in wood looked. However, he also continued to make figures that were meant to be coated with gesso, on into his late period. Among these were probably the two Angels holding Candlesticks. As a result of their multi-layered paint, they have lost their surface 'finish'. This may explain why they are more ruggedly yet crisply carved than the earlier Rothenburg figures.

18 Holy Bishop

Tilman Riemenschneider or workshop, *c.* 1505–10

From Burgebrach parish church (Bamberg Dist.)
Limewood (?), worked in the round, originally polychromed;
height: 89 cm
City of Würzburg, Inv. No. S. 44 737

This figure is in the round, made from a single block of wood without a hollowed back. The way the left hand pulls the cloak forward lends the figure its volume in full view although from the back it looks flat. Careful choice of wood, such as the core of a tree trunk, apparently ensured that the figure, although solid did not crack or split. Since the back has been worked and there are no traces of devices for fastening it there, the Bishop probably was a free-standing figure on a console. The figure is recorded in the inventory of the Gothic choir appointments of Burgebrach parish church. It may have originally been placed at the top of a winged altarpiece or flanked the altarpiece as a guardian of the shrine.

19 St Nicholas

Tilman Riemenschneider, *c.* 1510
Limewood (?), originally polychromed, hollowed back,
additions to crosier; height: 123 cm
City of Würzburg, Inv. No. S. 32 697

St Nicholas is represented dressed as a bishop in a cope and wearing a mitre. In his left hand he holds a crosier and in his right a book. On it three golden spheres were probably originally mounted which, in his charity, he gave to the three daughters of an impoverished nobleman as a dowry for each. The cope falls heavily over his body. Its deeply cleft folds, bunched in places, lend a high degree of plasticity to the figure. Nevertheless, the work looks self-contained since the upright figure steps only slightly forward onto the left foot and is meant to be viewed full face. Like St John Mourning (No. 16), St Nicholas, too, was originally destined for an altar shrine, as the hollowed back shows.

His face characterizes the saint as a wise, ascetic old man, gazing knowingly into the distance. Riemenschneider's ability to represent the psychology of his figures has often been admired. St Nicholas's countenance speaks eloquently of the master's way of playing with just a few details to evoke a certain mood and emotions. The skin of the saint's face is stretched tautly over his

Tombstone of Rudolf von Scherenberg (detail) Tilman Riemenschneider, 1496–99, Würzburg Cathedral

cheekbones and chin. The somewhat sunken cheeks, the deep wrinkles round the eyes and the nostrils show that age has caught up with St Nicholas. Nevertheless, the face expresses vitality: the eyebrows are forcefully knit together, the saint looks resolutely ahead as if he can see what the future holds. The elderly prince of the Church is a type frequently encountered in Tilman Riemenschneider's work, although the features accentuated vary widely. St Nicholas's head closely resembles that of the Prince-Bishop Rudolf von Scherenberg on his tomb in Würzburg Cathedral. Yet there the sunken mouth and flabby skin on the Prince-Bishop's cheeks and chin represent the transition from life to death. By contrast, St Nicholas's face is that of a still energetic man, smooth where the other face is merely slack.

The figure of St Nicholas was removed from Ehehalten House in Würzburg and added to the city art collections in 1882. From 1913 it was exhibited in the old museum building in Maxstrasse. After the building was gutted by fire in March 1945, it was feared that the figure had been destroyed. Then in 1950 the figure turned out to have been found by a man who had 'safeguarded' it. Presumably troubled by pangs of conscience, the 'finder' was induced to return the figure to the museum through an intermediary.

20

St Barbara

Tilman Riemenschneider or workshop, *c.* 1510

Limewood (?), originally polychromed, hollow back, additions
to chalice; height: 110 cm

City of Würzburg, Inv. No. S. 32 693

St Barbara wears a gown with a belt and, over them,
a wide cloak, which she has drawn across her body.
The veil, which has fallen forward from her neck to
form a narrow panel, lies in her hands. In her right
hand she is also holding her attribute, a chalice. Her
facial features are those characteristic of Riemenschneider's female figures as early as the Eve made for the
Würzburg Lady Chapel portal in 1492–9: an oval face
with almond-shaped eyes, a short, straight nose,
narrow lips and a dimpled chin (No. 3). The statue of
St Barbara was probably made in Riemenschneider's
workshop about 1510.

During the early years of the 16th century, the
Würzburg master received numerous important commissions. In 1501 the town of Rothenburg ob der
Tauber commissioned him to execute the Altarpiece
of the Holy Blood. Then in 1505 he received a commission for the high altar in Würzburg Cathedral and
another for the Altar of the Virgin in Creglingen.
Riemenschneider had also held public office from 1504
as a member of the Würzburg Lower Town Council.
Production on a large scale was possible in his workshop only because so many craftsmen worked in it.
Using models, they carved under the master's supervision. He himself often added the finishing touches
to a sculpture. With the standard upright figures that
were so much in demand for the shrines of simple
winged altarpieces, it is particularly difficult to distinguish between the master's work and that of his workshop.

21

Adoration of the Magi
Workshop of Tilman Riemenschneider, *c.* 1510

From Aub Castle chapel (Würzburg Dist.)

Limewood (?), originally polychromed, frame with back panel from a different context; height including frame: 103 cm; width including frame: 79 cm

Friends of Mainfrankish Art and History,
Inv. No. A. 32 703

The relief depicts the Virgin with the infant Christ on her lap in front of the manger at Bethlehem. The three wise men from the Orient are assembled before her. The eldest is already kneeling before the Virgin and has given her his gift in a covered spherical container. The other kings stand behind him, still holding the vessels they have brought with them.

The companion piece to this relief, depicting the birth of Christ, is in the Mainfränkisches Museum. The two panels were part of a winged altarpiece, where they were mounted on the inside of the shudders. Since the original frame is no longer extant, it is impossible to determine whether the reliefs were mounted one above the other on one side or on one winged panel each.

The Adoration scene derives from a copperplate engraving by Martin Schongauer (L. 6). The technique of print-making, introduced in the early 15th century, facilitated the production of multiple impressions. The Riemenschneider workshop was not the only one to use work by other artists as models. The Adoration scene, however, although considerably simplified and altered in details, is nearly a mirror image of the model.

Since Aub Castle was not built until the 17th century, the reliefs from its chapel, now in the Riemenschneider Collection, must have been destined for a different place, perhaps the winged altarpiece of the local parish church.

22

St Sebastian's hands (detail)

Workshop of Tilman Riemenschneider, *c.* 1515

Limewood (?), probably originally polychromed, hollowed back; overall height: 130 cm

City of Würzburg, Inv. No. S. 32 694

These hands, crossed and bound with rope at the wrists, are St Sebastian's. The wooden figure was made for the main body of an altarpiece, as the block-like composition and hollowed back indicate. Crisply carved throughout, and in this resembling the Main-fränkisches Museum's Angels with Candlesticks (No. 17), they may have been executed by a member of Riemenschneider's workshop. This ascription does not, however, detract from the quality of the figure.

The hands crossed over the lower torso are the focal point of the composition. They have been executed in such subtle and sensitive detail that the fingers and even the cuticles of the nails are rendered. The skin is stretched taut across the tendons and arteries on the backs of the hands, while the wrist-joints are prominent. For all this naturalism, the thin hands with their long fingers seem rather unreal. The anatomy of the hand has not been taken into consideration. Details seem as if they have been grasped in externals only. Insistence on naturalistic rather than realistic detail reveals that Riemenschneider and his workshop have not crossed the threshold between the Middle Ages and the Modern Age. Representation of the human body is based on precise observation, yet without benefit of a thorough grounding in anatomical studies, the salient factor differentiating Renaissance figure painting and sculpture from its Late Gothic antecedents.

23

Figures from a Holy Kinship

School of Tilman Riemenschneider, *c.* 1505–10

Limewood (?), with most of the original polychrome,
hollowed back; height: 113 and 118 cm

Friends of Mainfrankish Art and History,
Inv. No. H. 14 176

The two groups of figures (see illus. on pp. 62–63)
are turned toward each other. On the left are
Mary and Joseph; on the right, as their mirror images,
are Mary's mother Anne and Joachim. The youthful
Virgin originally held the infant Christ, who had
turned towards Anne. The composition of this group,
which was probably not produced in the Riemenschneider workshop, recalls representations of the
Holy Kinship from the hand of the Würzburg master.
Here, however, faces, hands and clothing are more
simply rendered.

Only a few sculptures in the Mainfränkisches Museum's Riemenschneider Collection have retained their original paint. This Holy Kinship, on which the rich gesso is still clearly visible, is a case in point. The outsides of cloaks and robes are brilliantly highlighted with gold leaf, originally enhanced by the shimmering colours of the lustre applied to the lining. The carnation of the faces was applied in multiple layers to give the women red cheeks and fresh complexions. The Virgin's gown, in dull azurite blue with appliqués of impressed brocade and gilt dots, contrasts sharply with her bright cloak.

Until well into the Riemenschneider era, wooden sculpture tended to be covered with gesso and paint. Carvers would hand on their work to painters, who painstakingly applied layer after layer of gesso compounded of costly ingredients. The gesso painters really defined the appearance of the finished work,

but since mixing and applying it was such a laborious and time-consuming process, gesso and paint were often more expensive than the sculpture itself.

All his working life, Tilman Riemenschneider produced both wood sculpture, which did not require elaborate painting, as well as sculpture made to be covered with multi-layered gesso in the traditional manner.

Detail of the Virgin's clothing: azurite blue with glued-on gilt paper dots and impressed brocade appliqués (metal appliqué designs, originally painted with coloured lacquer)

24

St Margaret

Brother Martinus Schwarz, *c.* 1485

From a chapel in Rothenburg ob der Tauber

Mixed media on conifer; height: 164 cm; width: 54 cm

Friends of Mainfrankish Art and History,
Inv. No. H. 14 258

St Margaret is depicted with the dragon at her feet against an incised gold ground. This panel was part of a winged altarpiece, destroyed in 1945 and said to have come from a chapel in Rothenburg ob der Tauber. A panel in the Mainfränkisches Museum depicting St Apollonia is its companion piece. Most of the original painting on the reverses has been lost.

The pattern incised in the gold ground identifies the painter of both panels as Martinus Schwarz of Rothenburg. Designs were made with stencils, which were reused repeatedly by workshops. The pomegranate pattern on the St Margaret panel is identical with the design on a hinged side panel from the Rothenburg Liebfrauen Altar, now in the Nuremberg Germanische Nationalmuseum. It was finished by the painter Martinus Schwarz, who had been recorded as a monk in the Rothenburg Franciscan monastery between 1485 and 1511. The St Margaret panel, with its identical pattern, may therefore be attributed to the same hand.

Like many of his contemporaries, Martinus Schwarz was both a painter and a sculptor. The pattern made by the impressed brocade decoration on clothing is often identical with the stencils used for the gold background of such panels, which suggests it was the work of a single workshop. Therefore, Riemenschneider must have collaborated with Brother Martinus Schwarz on the gesso figure groups of the Wibling Altarpiece now in the Munich Bayerisches Nationalmuseum.

Plain wood sculpture

25

Virgin and Child
Tilman Riemenschneider, *c.* 1510–15

Limewood, hollow back, originally with wood exposed;
height: 79 cm

On loan from private collection, Inv. No. Lg. 66 860

Several years ago, this Madonna was brought to the Mainfränkisches Museum to be examined by experts. She was still covered by up to 28 layers of paint. The figure is alleged to have always been in the same family. On Corpus Christi it adorned the house altar. Each year it used to be repainted for the occasion until its original appearance was no longer recognizable. On removing the paint from parts of the figure, the owners were amazed to find what was obviously a much older wooden sculpture than they had imagined. Experts at the Mainfränkisches Museum recognized its quality and its obvious similarities with Riemenschneider's work. Exhaustive study and careful restoration of the figure showed that it had not been painted originally. The Madonna had merely been coated with size under which details, such as pupils, brows, lips and cheeks, were tinted. Restored to its original condition with the wood showing through, the figure was revealed in all its masterly workmanship. The hair is meticulously carved, the faces subtly modulated and the seams and borders of clothing adorned with delicate designs. The exquisite carving suggests that Riemenschneider intended the work to be left unpainted because gesso and paint would have effaced his workmanship.

It is still unknown why the colouring of wood sculpture with gesso and paint suddenly became widely unpopular around 1490. Certainly plain wood sculpture emphasizes the art of carving so that now the sculptor rather than the painter had the last word. Since 1998 the City of Würzburg has been trying to secure the Madonna for the Museum.

26

Crucifix
Tilman Riemenschneider or workshop, c. 1515

Limewood (?), worked in the round, additions to left foot;
height: 57 cm
On loan from private collection, Inv. No. Lg. 66 920

The arms, which were originally attached by dowels, part of the right foot and the dangling ends of the loincloth are missing from this small crucifix. When the figure was recently restored, additions were made to the left foot to show the original proportions of the piece. Since the removal of several layers of the only partly preserved gesso, the fragment is again impressive for the consummate craftsmanship with which it was executed. Delicately chiselled hair, half-closed eyes, a slightly open mouth, straignt brows and narrow cheekbones characterize Christ who has just died. The ribcage and the veins and muscles of the legs are clearly delineated. Like the Virgin and Child described in the previous entry, this Christ Crucified was not originally covered with gesso. In places the original size has been preserved, which had protected details highlighted with colour. The blood trickling from the wounds on the figure's flanks and legs is still recognizably red.

Because its proportions are sturdier and the facial features are more tranquil than those of earlier crucifixes, the fragment is closer to the Würzburg Bürgerspital crucifix (No. 13). It was probably made about 1515 in Riemenschneider's workshop.

Like the Virgin and Child (No. 25), the present crucifix is also a recent rediscovery. Careful cleaning and restoration under the microscope have exposed the original surface and revealed its superb workmanship.

27

Double Madonna

Workshop of Tilman Riemenschneider, *c.* 1515–20

From St Barbara's Carmelite Church in Würzburg,
demolished in 1824

Limewood, two figures worked half in the round, originally
polychromed, additions to the iron ring; height: 90.5 cm

Friends of Mainfrankish Art and History,
Inv. No. A. 32 633

The work consists of two back-to-back figures, half in the round, of the Virgin standing in glory on a cloud base with the infant Christ on her arm. The contours of the figures correspond for the most part; however, the Christ Child's pose and the draping of the cloak differ slightly. The double Madonna was made to be suspended from the vaulting of a church. An aureole was probably mounted between the two halves of the figure, designating the Virgin in the sun as the Queen of Heaven. The figure may have hovered as a finial over a chandelier. In any case, it was mounted on a tenon as the original holes have been preserved.

The half made to be seen represents a type of Virgin common to the Riemenschneider workshop. The pose and position of the infant Christ as well as the texture of the cloak are roughly identical with those of the small, recently discovered Riemenschneider Virgin and Child (No. 25). However, the quality of workmanship is noticeably inferior in the double Madonna to the sophisticated, small statuette in the round, which may be due to its having been painted and then hung up far above eye-level. Lack of plasticity makes the curves of the face and body seem almost doughy, suggesting ascription to a member of the Riemenschneider workshop under the master's supervision.

28 St John Sleeping (detail)
Workshop of Tilman Riemenschneider, *c.* 1510
From the St Burchard Agony in the Garden group in Würzburg
Grey sandstone; overall height: 68 cm
City of Würzburg, Inv. No. S. 32 724

This figure is part of an Agony in the Garden group. In late medieval churches the scene on the Mount of Olives from the night before the Crucifixion was often reserved for outside niches. Christ was depicted kneeling in prayer while his disciples Peter, James and John slept and persecutors lurked in the background,

the whole tableau embedded in a landscape. Three such groups are known from the Riemenschneider workshop: on the church at Königheim near Tauberbischofsheim, the parish church of St Lawrence in Würzburg-Heidingsfeld and this one from the Würzburg Church of St Burchard. Originally placed in a niche flanking the west portal, the group was later moved to the north porch, only to be removed in 1830. For a time the figures stood in a vineyard on the Würzburg Nikolausberg until they were acquired by the city of Würzburg in 1907.

John is recumbent with his head laid on his bent

arm. His hand dangles limply. Erosion and damage have so altered the surface that little can be said about the workmanship. Nevertheless, the facial features are typical of Riemenschneider's work. The St Burchard Agony in the Garden figures were probably made in his workshop. In 1836 Karl Gottfried Scharold was the first to point out the group. He dated it to 1511, but failed to record a source so that the date cannot be verified. After sustaining severe damage in 1945, the figures, now restored, are in the Rittersaal of the Mainfränkisches Museum.

29

Virgin and Child

School of Tilman Riemenschneider, *c.* 1520–25

Limewood (?), hollow back, originally polychromed;
height: 140 cm

City of Würzburg, Inv. No. S. 49 743

This Virgin is of a type common to the Riemenschneider workshop, also represented by the double Madonna in the Mainfränkisches Museum (No. 27). The Virgin is depicted standing with the infant Christ in her arms. He clutches with both hands at her veil. The sculptor of this work was faithful to Riemenschneider's formal canon. Almond-shaped eyes, narrow lips and even the dimpled chin are all characteristic of the master's work. However, the squarehead of this figure and the flat, rugged carving lend it a very different appearance.

None of the many sculptures now attributed to Riemenschneider bears his signature. However, numerous records of commissions he received can be matched with extant sculpture so that a clear picture of his work emerges. Still only in Riemenschneider's early work is execution by his own hand assured. As he grew successful, Riemenschneider probably allowed his workshop to do more and more of the actual carving. A high turnover in workshop personnel was common even in the Middle Ages. When artisans left a workshop, they took types and techniques with them, assuring their dissemination. When an artist-craftsman was as successful as Riemenschneider, former colleagues would have worked in his manner for the rest of their careers. Nowadays work by artisans who trained in Riemenschneider's workshop and then left is designated as the 'Riemenschneider School', a term which might well apply to the maker of this Virgin and Child.

30 Tympanum with a Last Judgement

Circle of Tilman Riemenschneider, *c.* 1510

From the main portal of the first pilgrimage church in Dettelbach (Kitzingen Dist.)

Grey sandstone, severely eroded surface; height: 135 cm

Friends of Mainfrankish Art and History,
Inv. No. H. 14 350

Enthroned on the orb of the world, Christ the Judge dominates the middle of the tympanum, which depicts the Judgement Day. At his feet kneel the Virgin and John the Baptist, interceding for the dead who are portrayed in the lower zone of the tympanum as resurrected from their graves. They will either ascend to the Gates of Heaven with the Virgin or will descend to the depths of Hell behind John the Baptist. Three coats of arms adorn the lower frieze: in the centre the arms of the Prince-Bishop Lorenz von Bibra (tenure 1495–1519); on the left the arms of the town of Dettelbach and on the right those of an unknown burgher. The framing border bears a Latin inscription referring

to the representation of the Tribunal and the laying of the cornerstone of the old pilgrimage church in 1506.

By 1611 the church had been replaced by a new building. The old tympanum of the main portal was moved to the graveyard wall. In 1864 the town of Dettelbach presented it, already greatly eroded, to the

Lower zone of the tympanum with mason's mark and resurrected dead

Historischer Verein. From 1913 it was exhibited in the Würzburg Luitpold Museum. When the building was destroyed in 1945, the tympanum broke into numerous pieces and was not reassembled until 1998. Restoring the tympanum was like working on a giant puzzle, whose fragments were assembled on and affixed to a steel plate.

The mason's mark on the lower edge of the tympanum indicates the sculptor who executed it. Although his name is unknown, there are other works with this mark near Kitzingen. He was influenced by Riemenschneider's work although he probably worked independently. Nowadays the term for work by imitators is the 'Circle of Riemenschneider'.

31

Stone with Pankraz von Redwitz's coat of arms

Workshop of Tilman Riemenschneider, 1498

From the old Tannenberg Cathedral chapter house in Würzburg (now No. 2, Paradeplatz)

Grey sandstone with more recent polychrome; additions to the frame; height: 111.5 cm; width: 88.5 cm

City of Würzburg, Inv. No. S. 40 113

Very few secular works are known from the hand of Tilman Riemenschneider, who worked primarily for the Church. The Redwitz coat of arms, a table made for the Würzburg Town Hall (No. 32) and the woman decorating the Ochsenfurt chandelier (No. 33) number among the profane works assembled in the Riemenschneider Room of the Mainfränkisches Museum (see illus. on p. 4).

The coat of arms with the extensive helmet and heraldic decoration as well as the unicorn head, recalls Riemenschneider's work as a mason and was probably made in his workshop. According to the inscription, once on the upper border but destroyed in World War II, these are the armorial bearings of the Würzburg archdeacon Pankraz von Redwitz, who acquired Tannenberg Cathedral chapter house in 1498. The stone with the arms, set into the façade of the upper storey on the north side and visible from a great distance, identified the new owner. However, he did not live long to enjoy the chapter house, for he died the year he purchased it. The building remained in the Redwitz family until after 1509.

Tannenberg Cathedral chapter house was destroyed in 1945. After having the arms dug out of the ruins in pieces, the Mainfränkisches Museum acquired them in 1949.

32 Council Table

Tilman Riemenschneider, 1506

From the Würzburg Town Hall
Foot: oak; top: Solnhofen stone, originally polychromed;
the centre of the top composite, the rest restored; diameter
of top: 144 cm
City of Würzburg, Inv. No. S. 32 635

In 1506 Gabriel von Eyb, Bishop of Eichstätt, gave the city of Würzburg a slab of Solnhofen stone in return for Franconian wine with which the Würzburg Town Council had honoured him as a former dean of the Cathedral. The Council commissioned Tilman Riemenschneider to work the stone and make a pedestal. The top was to bear an inscription and the arms of the donor, Gabriel von Eyb, those of the Würzburg Prince-Bishop Lorenz von Bibra and the city of Würzburg. The armorial bearings were to be ordered so that 'when the table was cleared, each coat of arms would be on it'. Riemenschneider arranged the coats of arms round the centre of the round stone slab. The massive pedestal rises from three encapsulated hexagons. Three tracery arches lead into the actual pedestal at the centre, which is anchored in the innermost hexagon. The stone top is mounted on it in a wooden frame so that it can be turned. The field bearing the heraldic devices was originally coloured and gilt and the foot covered with green gesso. The inscription around the top was lost quite early on.

The Würzburg Town Hall table is a unique piece. There is nothing comparable to it among the few extant, showy pieces of Late Gothic furniture. This distinctive work of Tilman Riemenschneider shows the degree of imagination the master devoted to inventing new forms for unusual purposes.

33 Woman on a chandelier
Tilman Riemenschneider, *c.* 1515

From the Ochsenfurt am Main Town Hall
Bust: limewood (?), 20th-century polychromy,
antlers of a fourteen-pointer; height of bust: 57 cm
On loan from private collection, Inv. No. Lg. 62 173

This woman on a chandelier is one of the few extant secular room furnishings from Riemenschneider's hand. The speaking armorial bearings indicate that it was made for the town of Ochsenfurt, where a town hall was built in the late 15th century. The Council Chamber, for which the woman on a chandelier was probably commissioned, was finished in 1513.

Female busts decorating chandeliers were popular during the Middle Ages. They consisted of a bust and antlers, which carried the candle sockets. Two Riemenschneider chandeliers of this type are extant.

Tilman Riemenschneider's woman on a chandelier is his comment on the elegance of women's fashion of his day. The lady's coif expands like a halo above her thin face. She is wearing a flared gown with a fitted bodice and sleeves puffed at the elbows and wrists. A delicate chain round her neck disappears under her tucked-in kerchief, which is decorated with the letters 'AV • E • K'. The cruciform buttons on her bodice were carved separately and glued on. Her puffed sleeves were originally decorated with delicate piping, which was fastened at the top and bottom with tiny dowels. The presence of so

many intricately carved details may indicate that
the work was not intended to be coated with gesso.
Later, however, the lady on the chandelier fell victim
to the candles she bore. Modern painting covers
burnt spots on her left elbow.

34

Ecce Homo

Workshop of Tilman Riemenschneider, *c.* 1515

Limewood (?), worked in the round, originally probably
polychromed; height: 41 cm

City of Würzburg, Inv. No. S. 61 168

This little representation of Christ invested with the crown of thorns and the cloak by Pilat's henchmen represents a scene from the Passion heightened to an individual work. After the scourging, Christ was exposed to public mockery by Pontius Pilate with the words: 'Ecce homo – Behold the man'. Representations isolated such as this from a narrative context were used in the Middle Ages for contemplative private devotions and mystical meditation. In the 14th century most large-scale devotional statues were set up in churches, however, in the course of the 15th century they were increasingly removed to private chapels and households. With displacement came a reduction in scale.

This little Ecce Homo figure was intended for private devotions. It steps towards the spectator. The cloak framing it like a shell seems to open for a brief moment to expose the naked body under it to public view. The pose focuses our attention as do the intricately carved facial features suffused with an expression of suffering on a head disproportionately large for the body and the exaggeratedly large hands. One's gaze continually moves across the face, hands and body and round again. This is indeed a figure that inspires contemplative meditation.

Relatively little is known about medieval religious practices outside the church. Several of these intricately worked, small Riemenschneider statuettes are extant. Some of them are also thought to have served as models for large-scale figures (see No. 11).

35 Pietà (*Vesperbild*)

Workshop of Tilman Riemenschneider, *c.* 1510–15

From No. 10, Elefantengasse in Würzburg

Grey sandstone; height: 55.5 cm; width: 42 cm

City of Würzburg, Inv. No. S. 45 825

The relief depicts the Virgin seated before the Cross with Christ's body on her lap. Her right hand holds his head; the left grasps the veil that Mary seems to be about to use to dry her tears. Extrapolated from the iconography of the Lamentation after the Descent from the Cross, in Germany a scene of this type is called a Vesperbild after the Good Friday custom of contemplating at Vespers the five sacred wounds of the dead Christ lying across his mother's knees. The Pietà, meaning 'pity' in Italian, or the Vesperbild was also used for private devotions of a meditative nature.

This relief from the house at No. 10, Elefantengasse in Würzburg was probably made in the Riemenschneider workshop. In Riemenschneider's day, the courtyard there was owned by the Ganzhorn family, whose coat of arms is depicted in the lower left-hand corner of the relief. The work may have been commissioned for a tomb in nearby St Peter's churchyard to commemorate a member of the family who had died. However, since the family coat of arms need not designate a specific member of the family, the relief could just as easily have been inlaid in a wall in a domestic context as a private devotional image.

36 – 38

Three papier mâché Pietàs (*Vesperbilder*)

Workshop of Tilman Riemenschneider, *c.* 1515

Papier mâché, several layers of overpainting;
height: 37 cm and 33 cm

City of Würzburg, Inv. No. Lg. 67 000, S. 43 608,
S. 47 577

These three Pietàs or Vesperbilder resemble in detail that in the Ganzhorn family relief (No. 35). However, because these are in low relief, the heads are viewed frontally. All three of these low reliefs are made of papier mâché. Two of them are the same size; they were later placed in a glass case and are today coated with brown varnish. They were made from a mould produced in the Riemenschneider workshop. The third relief is probably a smaller-scale replica of one of the larger pieces.

Workshops easily made large numbers of such reliefs by pressing them from a mould like that used to form baked goods. Presumably they were used in private devotions as replicas of miraculous images, which their owners had venerated on pilgrimages.

39

Virgin and Child
Tilman Riemenschneider, *c.* 1520
From Würzburg
Grey sandstone with traces of old polychrome;
height: 155 cm
City of Würzburg, Inv. No. S. 46 672

Slightly smaller than life-size, the figure of the Virgin is depicted frontally. Despite being only about 25 cm thick, the sculpture gives an impression of great depth. This effect is produced largely by the subtle play of staggered planes, creating an illusion of foreshortening between foreground and background. The front plane is articulated by the discontinuous lines of the folds, suggesting that the cloak is of thick fabric. The sinuous texture of the material beneath the cloak is visible only in the plinth zone. With his right hand the infant Christ reaches behind his mother's neck while his left draws her veil into the foreground. Thus the folds of the Virgin's cloak frame the faces of mother and child in a circle expressive of affectionate intimacy.

The reductive repose with which the sweep of the folds is suggested and the uniformly soft modulation of the faces, suffused with an expression of gentle melancholy, indicate that this stone sculpture was made by Riemenschneider in old age. The heads in the Maidbronn Lamentation relief are similar. A late work of Riemenschneider, a stone figure of the Virgin now in the Frankfurt Liebig House, represents a mirror image of the composition of the Würzburg Virgin and Child.

Made in Würzburg, the Madonna was owned by the sculptor Andreas Halbig (1807–69) until 1869.

He lived in the Hauger Deanery, where the figure may have been in devotional use. It may originally have come from the old Hauger chapter church. When the medieval church was demolished in 1657, the figure may have passed to the deanery.

40

St Stephen

Tilman Riemenschneider, *c.* 1520–25

Limewood (?), originally polychromed, hollow back;
height: 76 cm

Friends of Mainfrankish Art and History,
Inv. No. H. 14 063

Portrayed as a youthful figure, St Stephen is dressed as a deacon. The saint was one of the seven deacons appointed by the Apostles in Jerusalem. Forceful and eloquent in spreading the Christian faith, he was condemned to death by the Sanhedrin in Jerusalem and stoned. To indicate the manner of the saint's martyrdom, Riemenschneider has set three stones on the right leg of the seated figure. The back of the sculpture has been hollowed out, therefore it was probably made for an altarpiece, where it is likely to have stood in the predella or plinth.

The large, closed form, the quiet flow of the figure's garments and the face, an established type of the raptly contemplative, are all characteristic of Riemenschneider's late work. A legend has persisted that the master's hands were broken when he was held captive for nine weeks in Marienberg in 1525. During the Peasants' Revolt, Riemenschneider sided with the rebels. As a member of the Würzburg Town Council, he refused to bear arms in the service of the Prince-Bishop. His work for the Benedictine convent in Kitzingen in 1527 is documented. Therefore, Riemenschneider was certainly able to carve after his release from prison. However, the Peasants' Revolt marked the end of the era of large winged altarpieces in Franconia as elsewhere. The region was so impoverished that works could no longer be commissioned on such a lavish scale. Moreover, the Renaissance ushered in a taste for different forms. By the time Riemenschneider died in 1531, his work was considered outdated, which explains why the master was so quickly forgotten by posterity.

41

Four saints from a Fourteen Holy Helpers relief (detail)

In the style of Tilman Riemenschneider, c. 1530

From the chapel in the Hofspital in Würzburg

Limewood (?), originally polychromed; overall height: 57 cm

City of Würzburg, Inv. No. S. 40 120

The clothing and attributes of the figures portrayed in this detail enable one to identify St Margaret with a book, St Eustace with a stag's head, St Barbara with a chalice and, presumably, Acacius. They form part of a relief depicting the Fourteen Holy Helpers. Representations of the fourteen martyrs were widespread from the early 14th century, uniting saints whose intercession was efficacious in times of need. The relief in the Mainfränkisches Museum came from the Würzburg Hofspital chapel, which was consecrated to the Fourteen Holy Helpers, and was probably made for the predella of a winged altarpiece.

Although the facial features suggest Riemenschneider's influence, the heads of these figures are indeed round by comparison with his. Furthermore, the hairstyles and clothing depicted are no longer those of Riemenschneider's day. St Eustace wears a grooved breastplate of a type that did not become fashionable until about 1510. St Margaret's plaited coiffure is from the same period. The cap on St Eustace's head appears, albeit in a simplified form, on Riemenschneider's own tombstone (No. 1). Looking as if a 'fresh breeze' has animated what may have been characteristic of an elderly sculptor whose work has long since lapsed into routine, this relief may well be the work of his son Jörg, who took over the Riemenschneider workshop after his father's death. Ascription to another young member of the Riemenschneider workshop would be equally plausible. Research has yet to shed light on the influence exerted by Riemenschneider's work on the generation of artists who succeeded him. Their subject matter and aesthetic values already seem remote from the old master's world view.

Bibliography

Justus Bier, *Tilman Riemenschneider:*
Die frühen Werke, Würzburg, 1925.
–, *Tilman Riemenschneider:*
Die reifen Werke, Augsburg, 1930.
–, *Tilman Riemenschneider:*
Die späten Werke in Stein, Vienna, 1973.
–, *Tilman Riemenschneider:*
Die späten Werke in Holz, Vienna, 1978.

Hanswernfried Muth, *Tilman Riemenschneider:*
Die Werke des Bildschnitzers und Bildhauers, seiner
Werkstatt und seines Umkreises im Mainfränki-
schen Museum Würzburg, catalogue of the collection,
vol. 1, Würzburg, 1982.

Tilman Riemenschneider: Frühe Werke, catalogue of the
exhibition in the Mainfränkisches Museum Würzburg
mounted jointly by the Sculpture Galery of the
Staatliche Museen Preussischer Kulturbesitz Berlin,
the City of Würzburg and the region of Lower Franconia,
5 Sept.–1 Nov. 1981, Berlin, 1981.

Front cover: Virgin and Child, Tilman Riemenschneider, *c.* 1500,
(detail), see p. 31

Back cover (top): Angel holding a Candlestick, Workshop
of Tilman Riemenschneider, *c.* 1505. Mainfränkisches Museum,
Würzburg; (bottom): St Sebastian's hand (detail), workshop
of Tilman Riemenschneider, *c* 1505

Photos: Rolf Nachbar, Reichenberg, except for
p. 50: Georg Christ, Würzburg;
p. 44: Karl Halbauer, Stuttgart;
p. 8, 9 (middle): Toni Schneiders, Lindau

© Prestel-Verlag, Munich · London · New York

Prestel-Verlag · 26 Mandlstrasse · 80802 Munich
Tel. 089/381709-0 · Fax 089/381709-35

Translated from the German by Joan Clough-Laub
Edited by Michele Schons
Photoset and design by Norbert Dinkel, Munich
Lithography by Eurocrom 4, Villorba
Printed by Peradruck, Munich
Bound by Attenberger, Munich

Printed in Germany on acid-free paper
ISBN 3-7913-2211-7